STAR BIOGRAPHIES

MILLIE BOBBY
BROWN

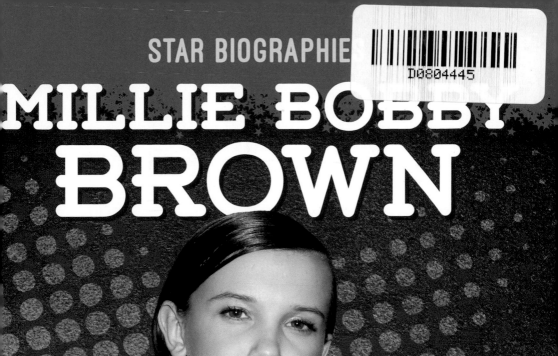

KENNY ABDO

Fly!
An Imprint of Abdo Zoom
abdobooks.com

abdobooks.com

Published by Abdo Zoom, a division of ABDO, P.O. Box 398166, Minneapolis,
Minnesota 55439. Copyright © 2019 by Abdo Consulting Group, Inc. International
copyrights reserved in all countries. No part of this book may be reproduced in any
form without written permission from the publisher. Fly!™ is a trademark and logo
of Abdo Zoom.

Printed in the United States of America, North Mankato, Minnesota.
092018
012019

THIS BOOK CONTAINS
RECYCLED MATERIALS

Photo Credits: Alamy, AP Images, Everette Collection, Getty Images, iStock, newscom,
Shutterstock, ©Netflix p14/Kobal/Shutterstock, ©Gage Skidmore p16 CC BY-SA 2.0
Production Contributors: Kenny Abdo, Jennie Forsberg, Grace Hansen
Design Contributors: Dorothy Toth, Neil Klinepier

Library of Congress Control Number: 2018946310

Publisher's Cataloging-in-Publication Data

Names: Abdo, Kenny, author.
Title: Millie Bobby Brown / by Kenny Abdo.
Description: Minneapolis, Minnesota : Abdo Zoom, 2019 | Series: Star biographies
    | Includes online resources and index.
Identifiers: ISBN 9781532125478 (lib. bdg.) | ISBN 9781641856928 (pbk) |
    ISBN 9781532126499 (ebook) | ISBN 9781532127007 (Read-to-me ebook)
Subjects: LCSH: Brown, Millie Bobby, 2004- --Juvenile literature. | Actors--
    United States--Biography--Juvenile literature. | Television actors and
    actresses--Biography--Juvenile literature. | Fashion models--Biography—
    Juvenile literature.
Classification: DDC 791.45092 [B]--dc23

TABLE OF CONTENTS

MILLIE BOBBY
BROWN

Millie Bobby Brown is a young star who has turned the entertainment world upside down with her superhuman talent!

In her short career, she has taken TV shows, music videos, and the fashion industry by storm.

EARLY YEARS

Millie Bobby Brown was born in Marbella, Andalucia, Spain in 2004.

Brown has a big family. She has three siblings. Her family moved from Spain to England when she was four years old.

Brown and her family then moved to Orlando, Florida, when she was eight. There, she could follow her dream of acting.

THE BIG TIME

Brown got her big break in 2013. She starred in an episode of *Once Upon a Time in Wonderland* as Young Alice. She went on to guest star on shows like *NCIS*, *Modern Family*, and *Grey's Anatomy*.

Brown landed her most **iconic role** in 2016. She played super-powered runaway, Eleven, on *Stranger Things*. The show was a worldwide sensation and she received critical praise.

The second season of *Stranger Things* came out in 2017. Again, it was a smash hit. Brown racked up more **acclaim** and award **nominations** reprising her **role** as Eleven.

Brown made her big-screen **debut** in 2019 when she starred in *Godzilla: King of Monsters*.

LEGACY

Brown was **nominated** for an Outstanding Supporting Actress in a Drama Series award at the 2017 Primetime Emmy's. She is one of the youngest people to do so.

She was named one of the 100 most **influential** people in the world by TIME magazine in 2018. Brown is the youngest person to ever be included on the list!

21

GLOSSARY

acclaim – public and enthusiastic praise.

debut – a first appearance.

icon – a person who is seen as a representative symbol of something.

influential – someone who has a strong influence over people or things.

nomination – proposing someone for an honor or award.

role – a part an actor plays.

ONLINE RESOURCES

Booklinks
NONFICTION NETWORK
FREE! ONLINE NONFICTION RESOURCES

To learn more about Millie Bobby Brown, please visit **abdobooklinks.com**. These links are routinely monitored and updated to provide the most current information available.

INDEX